(c) 2018 Kathleen Rodir  rights reserved.

No part of this book may be reproduced, scanned, or distributed in any printed, mechanical, or electronic form (including recording or photocopying) without written permission, except in the case of brief quotations embodied in critical articles or reviews. Every effort has been made to ensure that the information contained in this book is complete and accurate. However, neither the publisher nor the author is rendering professional advice or services to the individual reader. Neither the author nor the publisher shall be liable or responsible for loss or damage allegedly arising from any information or suggestion in this book.

All rights reserved for translation into foreign languages.

ISBN: 978-0692165942

Requests for permissions should be addressed to the author at Oily Baa-lievers, 2751 Springfield Street, Bismarck, North Dakota 58503, or via email at RebootNow14@gmail.com.

Printed in the United States of America

REBOOT

Release Emotions and Remember
Wholeness
Using Essential Oils

by KATHLEEN RODIN

Bulk Discounts

My goal is to get this publication into the hands of as many people as possible for their personal development and emotional well-being. To make this goal a reality, I am offering a bundle discount program that will allow business leaders to have copies of *Reboot* on hand at all times. **I encourage you to invest in the personal development and emotional health of your entire organization by gifting** *Reboot* **to:**

- <u>Every</u> **leader currently in your organization**
- <u>Every</u> **person who joins your organization in the future**
- **Make copies of Reboot available for purchase at all your classes and events**

1 copy of Reboot @ $9.95 = $9.95 USD
5 copies of Reboot @ $9.50 = $47.50 USD
10 copies of Reboot @ $9.00 = $90.00 USD
25 copies Reboot @ $8.50 = $212.50 USD
50 copies Reboot @ $8.00 = $400.00 USD
100 copies Reboot @ $7.50 = $750.00 USD
250 copies Reboot @ $7.00 = $1,750.00 USD

For ordering in bulk quantities or for any questions, please contact us at RebootNow14@gmail.com.

Please contact us by email if you are interested in scheduling the author for a speaking engagement or a *Reboot* event.

Disclaimer

As with anything, there are differing opinions among experts, reference guides, and everyday essential oil users. This information represents what I, as an Independent Distributor of Young Living Essential Oils, have chosen to do to take charge of my own personal emotional health and does not represent Young Living. I am not a doctor. Even though I have used essential oils safely for six years, I am not an essential oils expert. Statements in this publication have not been evaluated by the Food and Drug Administration. Products that are mentioned in *Reboot* are not intended to diagnose, treat, cure, or prevent any disease. If you are pregnant, nursing, taking medication, or have a medical condition, consult your physician before using the oils mentioned in *Reboot*. Information found in this publication is meant for educational and informational purposes only, and to motivate you to make your own physical and emotional healthcare decisions based upon your own *further* research and in partnership with your healthcare provider. The information in this publication should not be relied upon to determine a medical diagnosis or courses of treatment.

Young Living Essential Oils

I am proud to be a Young Living Independent Distributor. I only use and recommend Young Living essential oils because of their calling and promise of purity known as Seed to Seal®. With Young Living, there are non-negotiable benchmarks for delivering a product that members can feel confident about. They are multifaceted, exacting, and—above all—concrete. Young Living offers an extensive line of authentic, essential oil-infused solutions that represent the best of nature—all purity, no compromises—through the standards of their groundbreaking Seed to Seal® program. Young Living's sourcing, science and standards are incomparable. **Choose Young Living for 100% pure, therapeutic-grade essential oils!**

The Essential Oils Desk Reference

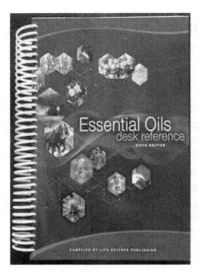

Reboot is similar to *"Letting Go" with Essential Oils* of the Essential Oils Desk Reference (EODR). It states, "This is a very simple guideline for "letting go" of some old emotional baggage, releasing, allowing the up-lifting feeling of peace and emotional freedom to take root." The EODR can be purchased from Life Science Publishing at www.discoverlsp.com. If you would like to do your own research and learn more about the essential oils in *Reboot*, consider purchasing this valuable resource.

Reboot has been written for everyone, but believers in Jesus Christ will find that the verbiage has been modified and includes over 100 Biblical scriptures so they will feel comfortable with the language used while participating. These language modifications will also put believers at ease when inviting other Christians to participate without feeling as if they are compromising their biblical beliefs and standards. Great God and great oils!

However, even if you do not hold to a Christian belief, *Reboot's* affirmations in the *Reaffirm* sections will resonate strongly with you. I pray God would be glorified and everyone will experience emotional release and freedom.

Reboot also serves as your own personal journal. The Reflect section has been designed to give participants a small space to date and record their emotional release experiences several times. For those who would like to expound and need more space, consider recording your experiences in a journal. Watch for the *Reboot* journal coming soon!

About the Author - Kathleen K. Rodin

At an incredibly young age, I witnessed violent, physical abuse in my home because of my father's alcohol abuse. This eventually led to the divorce of my parents and my father leaving our home, all of which were very traumatic to me. The middle of five children, physically abandoned by my father and emotionally abandoned by my traumatized, overwhelmed, and brokenhearted mother (she did the best she knew how), I "managed" my fear and trauma by hiding. In the years that followed, I believed I was alone, invisible, and insignificant. My perception of myself was that I didn't matter, and that nobody cared about me. Believing these false perceptions to be true, I became an angry, rebellious, out-of-control addict, repeating the cycles of craziness, even though I swore I wouldn't. My mother recognized my cries for help (she wasn't as absent as I thought) and put me in a treatment facility for alcohol addiction the summer before my senior year of high school. I completed treatment, finished high school at mid-year and moved to a city approximately 40 miles from my hometown.

I was excited for the next chapter of my life. However, my tool belt for life was empty and shortly after, I relapsed. Within three months, I was at my lowest. I literally hit rock-bottom and while under the influence of alcohol, made a suicidal gesture. I entered treatment a second time at the age of 18, on June 21, 1981. I began attending Alcoholics Anonymous (AA) meetings after I was discharged from treatment. It was there, I met and became attracted to a man much older than I (which I now realize was my attempt to fill the void of my absent father and my absent Father, God). I became pregnant and we were married when our daughter was a year old. He was also a recovering alcoholic and physically and emotionally abusive. We divorced approximately one year after the birth of our second daughter. I moved back to my hometown with my 4-year-old and 9-month-old daughters and began a new life with them.

Working as a waitress at the local cafe, I met a kind and wonderful man who ate breakfast, lunch, and supper at the cafe nearly every day. We were married a year and a half, and our daughter was born ten months later. We were and still are faithful in attending weekly worship services as believers in Jesus and have been married for

33 years at the time of this publication. By the grace of God, I have been sober "one day at a time "for 40 years.

Even though I was sober, I still suffered off and on from depression and anxiety for many years. The alcohol was removed, but I continued to choose old patterns (stuffing emotions, people-pleasing, trying to be perfect) subconsciously dictated by childhood trauma, teenage rebellion and guilt and shame from poor choices I had made. I was in bondage. I was also unknowingly teaching these unhealthy patterns of coping with life to my daughters. I too, like my mom, was doing the best I knew how. It wasn't until many years later, when I walked out of a stressful job, physically and emotionally burned out, that I discovered Young Living Essential Oils. Honestly, I didn't know then, that God would use *that* first purchase of the YL Oils Premium Starter Kit as an instrument in my seemingly, unconquerable quest for emotional freedom. I know now that it was always in God's divine plan that led me *to* them, and *to* the Young Living team I am on.

"For I know the plans I have for you," declares the Lord, "plans to prosper you and not to harm you, plans to give you hope and a future." Jeremiah 29:11.

His plan was and is emotional freedom...yours and mine...and His plan includes this book...***Reboot***!

Endorsements

"I just have to say this book is amazing. I love how Kathleen has connected all the dots to emotions, oils, the Bible, and science. What a breath of fresh air! Read the pages, answer the questions and find yourself remembering wholeness now!"

~ Dr. Sharnael Wolverton-Sehon,
Naturopathic Doctor and Minister
Swiftfire Ministries International - www.swiftfire.org

"I love this book! It is written with such simplicity, yet it is so profound in the richness of what Kathleen shares regarding essential oils and emotions. We are spirit beings who have a soul and live in a body. We all have emotions, and this book teaches us how to process them through our words, thoughts, actions, the use of essential oils, and God's Word to promote wholeness and well-being. You will find so many ways to incorporate this book into your life; use this book for your own personal journey and growth, in Bible studies, in your essential oil classes, family devotions and much more! Get creative! Thank you, Kathleen, for writing this book and sharing your knowledge with the world! I'm excited to get several copies to share with my family and friends!"

~ Carrie Raab, Young Living Gold

"This is a must-have book for anyone wanting to begin their emotional wellness journey with essential oils. Kathleen has laid everything out beautifully and just by reading this book you feel a release of emotions and sense of peace. I am excited to use this book in my own personal journey and in my classes. What an amazing resource for anyone!"

~ Billie Cornell, Wellness Coach & Educator

Foreword

"If 'old things have passed away and all things have become new' at salvation, why am I still struggling?" In my years of pastoral counseling and prayer ministry, I have heard this question many times. I have shed countless tears with victims of sexual, emotional, physical, verbal, spiritual and ritual abuse, as they wondered why the wounds in their souls did not vanish when they were born again.

My quest for answers, both for others and for myself, started me on a journey of exploration concerning the way God has created us in His image: spirit, soul, and body. We are spirit-beings, who have souls and live in bodies. At salvation, our spirits (the real and eternal part of us) is made complete and new in Him and we are now of a different bloodline - no longer of the DNA of Adam, but of the DNA of our Father, God! The process of spiritual growth is basically that of "working out our salvation with fear and trembling" (Philippians 2:12). This involves "pulling down strongholds" (II Corinthians 10:4) and being "transformed by the renewing of our mind" (Romans 12:2). We are literally being changed "from glory to glory" (II Corinthians 3:18) as we allow what has already happened in our spirits to work its way out into our souls, our bodies and into the earth.

I am thankful that Kathleen has written this book, because, over the years, I have seen many believers remain stuck in repetitive cycles of rejection, fear, depression, addiction, pain, failure, and physical infirmity simply because they did not understand how to co-labor with the Lord in this process of the restoration of the soul. Sometimes we are afraid to revisit the past or are ashamed of the things we have done or experienced. Often, we repress traumatic memories, only to find that the root, though buried, continues resonating pain from the subconscious and unconscious layers of the soul, producing negative fruit. It is true that "... as a man thinks in his heart (even those deep, unconscious layers), so is he" (Proverbs 23:7). Many times, we are what James 1:8 calls "double minded." The conscious parts of our minds and emotions desire love, success, and victory, and yet the unhealed places within us continue to create the opposite. Our Father loves us and is not withholding any good thing from us (Psalm 84:11). He desires "truth in the inward parts" (Psalm 51:6) simply because He wants us to be whole - fully aligned to receive His limitless blessings.

Kathleen is a beautiful soul and someone that I felt instantly and deeply connected to the moment we first spoke. She is well qualified to write this book, because she has experienced deep pain and trauma herself and has allowed the Holy Spirit to bring her into a place of healing and victory. As someone who has suffered much, she will impart to you great compassion, depth, and insight. And as someone who has overcome, she will impart authority, along with practical keys and powerful strategies for victory. I love the way Kathleen combines wisdom, intuition, science, the Word of God, and natural, earthly gifts like essential oils to display the Father's Divine tapestry of healing.

We know from Scripture that, because of the cross, the enemy has been stripped of his usurped authority and that he possesses no creative ability; he simply "steals, kills and destroys" what God has created for His children (John 10:10). Many believers have unknowingly rejected some beautiful gifts of God because they have seen the stolen or counterfeited versions and have been afraid that using essential oils or understanding the way God's life (energy) flows through our bodies is New Age or occult. This book is so needed to help believers understand the Scriptural basis for these things, so that we can receive them, benefit from them, and freely enjoy all that that Father has created for our good.

Often, we hear truths that rivet our hearts, yet have difficulty knowing how to apply them to our lives. That will not be the case with this book! Kathy has made even the deepest concepts very easy to understand and has created a practical format that will walk you through exactly how to apply what you are learning to your specific situation. If you read and work through this book with an open heart, you will be changed. You will begin to see negative cycles in your life with fresh vision and will know exactly how to release trauma from your soul and your body. Even if you are already familiar with essential oils or have already experienced a measure of healing in your soul, this will be a book that you will want to revisit again and again… as you go higher in intimacy with the King and as He goes deeper and deeper in you."

**Virginia Killingsworth, Senior leader, All Things Restored Church
Worship leader, Recording Artist, Bible Teacher & Speaker,
(www.virginiakillingsworth.com)
Essential Oil Junkie & Wellness Enthusiast (www.lifeunlimited.life)**

Personal Dedications

I dedicate this publication first to my Lord and Savior, Jesus Christ who paid the ultimate price to bring the Father glory and to lift me out of a deep, dark pit. Your love is completely satisfying, and I know that I am valued and forever belong to your family. *"Praise be to the God and Father of our Lord Jesus Christ, who has blessed us in the heavenly realms with every spiritual blessing in Christ. For he chose us in him before the creation of the world to be holy and blameless in his sight. In love, He predestined us for adoption to sonship through Jesus Christ, in accordance with his pleasure and will—to the praise of his glorious grace, which he has freely given us in the One he loves."* Ephesians 1:3-6.

Second, to my kind, devoted and steadfast husband, Dennis. Thank you for your Christ-like love, faithfulness, support <u>and for staying</u>. You have lived out Ephesians 5:25-28 well, *"Husbands, love your wives, just as Christ loved the church and gave himself up for her to make her holy, cleansing her by the washing with water through the word, and to present her to himself as a radiant church, without stain or wrinkle or any other blemish, but holy and blameless. In this same way, husband's ought to love their wives as their own bodies. He who loves his wife loves himself."*

Third, I would like to dedicate this to my three daughters, Meagan, Amanda, and Emily. I love you all so much and my hope for each of you is that you always passionately love and serve God and care for each other. *"I have no greater joy than to hear that my children are walking in the truth."* 3 John 1:4.

Fourth, I would like to dedicate this to my dear friend, prayer partner and sister in Christ, Bonnie. I asked for wisdom which God has freely given, plus He gave me a wise friend. And He sent you in one of my darkest hours. I treasure our friendship. *"If any of you lacks wisdom, you should ask God, who gives generously to all without finding fault, and it will be given to you."* James 1:5. *"Plans fail for lack of counsel, but with many advisers, they succeed."* Proverbs 15:22.

Lastly, I dedicate this publication to all those who are searching for emotional freedom. *"Ask and it will be given to you; seek and you will find; knock and the door will be opened to you. For everyone who asks receives; the one who seeks finds; and to the one who knocks, the door will be opened." Matthew 7:7-8. Keep* knocking *until the door opens. Keep **Reboot**ing until you are fearless and free!*

Special Dedication

This book and the expertly blended essential oils in **Reboot** would not be available to you and me if it weren't for the dedication, pioneering spirit, love, and wisdom of one man; D. Gary Young. Described by many as a modern pioneer, inventor, and historian, Gary's pursuit of new wellness discoveries was rooted in ancient practices as he attempted to unlock and share the benefits bestowed by creation. His determination to achieve physical and emotional well-being, combined with his lifelong love of nature, drove him to learn everything about essential oils. He traveled the globe in search of aromatic plants that would offer therapeutic wholeness to the world. His legacy will continue to be carried on Mary Young and by millions of people who have embraced the Young Living lifestyle and have promised to journey on. I am so grateful to God for D. Gary Young and Young Living!

"The Spirit of the Sovereign LORD is on me, because the LORD has anointed me to proclaim good news to the poor. He has sent me to bind up the brokenhearted, to proclaim freedom for the captives and release from darkness for the prisoners, to proclaim the year of the LORD's favor and the day of vengeance of our God, to comfort all who mourn, and provide for those who grieve in Zion—to bestow on them a crown of beauty instead of ashes, the oil of joy instead of mourning, and a garment of praise instead of a spirit of despair. They will be called oaks of righteousness, a planting of the LORD for the display of his splendor."
Psalm 61:1-3.

How it All Began

I have been a singer most of my life. I sang at home, at school, at events, in choirs and I was a member of the church praise team. I sang solos, duets, trios, and in small and large groups. Sometime people would say a few words and I could instantly start singing a song with those words. Music has been a joy to me, and I would say that I come from a musically inclined family. But six and a half years ago, in a dark time of my life, I quit singing. Not because I wanted to, but because I couldn't. For months, I literally could not think of a song or the words of a song to sing. I wanted to sing, but I just couldn't seem to.

As I was paging through my reference guide for essential oils, I noticed a page that contained information about using essential oils on the ears to release emotions. It was called Auricular Emotional Therapy. I noticed there were oils indicated to use for anger, hate and fear, all of which I was dealing with at this time in my life. There were also oils indicated to use if you had mother or father issues, depression, self-pity, guilt and more. I was fairly new to the world of essential oils and was pleased to see that in the short time I was a Young Living member, I had three of the fifteen oils listed on the diagram; so, I applied Valor, Release and Joy on two locations of each ear. About an hour later, as I was home alone doing dishes, I "heard" myself singing! I was shocked! I didn't even know I was singing; the words of the song were just pouring out of me without thinking. It was like the floodgates poured life-giving water on my parched soul! I was singing! Even more surprising was that I was singing the words to a familiar hymn, *"Perfect submission, all is at rest. I in my Savior am happy and blest."* This was when I realized that the essential oils, I had purchased weren't just for *smelling* good but also for ***feeling*** good.

My second experience with using essential oils for emotional release was led by my sister while she was visiting from Texas. She had purchased and brought with her, twelve essential oils for an emotional release protocol outlined in a reference guide. At one point during the protocol, I had a memory surface of a childhood best friend who did not come to say good-bye to me when I moved away from my childhood home at the age of 10. I realized this was one of the deep roots, fed from the well of abandonment, that caused me to continue to feel unimportant and invisible. I carried this feeling of being insignificant for much of my life. As this memory was brought to my awareness, the therapeutic benefits of the essential oils helped me peacefully remember and easily release the pain from this memory. At the completion of the emotional release protocol, I remember feeling treasured, loved and at peace.

Over a period of a few months, I purchased all the emotional release oils on my Young Living Essential Rewards wholesale member account, so I could do the emotional release protocol with my own oils. *(Note: See Appendix 4 on pages 70-71 to find out how you can purchase all the Young Living Essential Oils used in Reboot as a wholesale member of Young Living through Essential Rewards).*

Now, with the addition of my own emotional release oils in my toolbelt, I did the emotional release protocol for a third time. When I applied and breathed in the aroma of the oil blend of Forgiveness, I began to recall with the help of the Holy Spirit, several people who I felt *compelled* to forgive. I simply began saying the words quietly, but audibly, "I forgive _____. Over and over, names of people I had harbored unforgiveness towards came to my mind. I did this until I had exhausted a long list.

True forgiveness begins by realizing that we too have been forgiven. Colossians 3:14 says, *"Bear with each other and forgive one another if any of you has a grievance against someone. Forgive as the Lord forgave you."* Choose to forgive and set *yourself* free. I do not recall that I had any outward manifestations of emotional release but remember that I experienced the same feelings of deep love and peace as I concluded the emotional release protocol. Les Brown said, *"Forgive anyone who has caused you pain or harm. Keep in mind that forgiving is not for others. It is for you. Forgiving is not forgetting. It is remembering without anger. It frees up your power, heals your body, mind, and spirit. Forgiveness opens up a pathway to a new place of peace where you can persist despite what has happened to you."*

My fourth emotional release experience consisted quickly applying the *Reboot* oils before heading out the door for a chiropractic appointment. I had a good adjustment or a physical release that morning in my mid-back. As I drove home, I suddenly began crying and continued to cry for another thirty minutes when I got home. I didn't try to stop myself from crying and I don't recall that I was able to identify any specific feeling, emotion, or traumatic event. It just felt good to cry and to let the emotion go. It was loud and a little ugly. I knew that I was responding to the essential oils I had used that morning. I was releasing emotion(s). This emotional release experience, like the others was therapeutically cleansing and freeing.

Shortly after this, God began to lay it on my heart to extend an invitation to other people to experience the same, therapeutic, emotional release protocol in my home. One of my friends, a Christian woman, responded to my invitation. As I led her through *Reboot* using the essential oils, she had a really good experience and at one point told me of a vision she had. Her experience was so positive, she purchased the Oils Starter Bundle before going home. In a follow-up call, she told me that she shared her experience with her husband and showed him the copy of the emotional release page I'd sent with her. Unfortunately, he admonished her, believing that the language and protocol was *new age.* Out of fear of doing something wrong and in obedience to her husband, she put her brand-new bundle away. I was grieved in my spirit, sad and shaken (familiar spirit of fear). This caused me to *briefly* doubt the use of essential oils for emotions and prevented me for a short time in doing it or inviting others to. If honest, I had to admit that I was uncomfortable with some of the words used in the protocol too. The word "chakras" was unfamiliar to me as a Christian, so I looked for trusted sources to help me understand this and other words. One article that was of immense help to me was, "Are Chakras New Age?" by pastor and author Dr. David Stewart. He writes that chakras are *"electromagnetic centers along the spine of our EM (electromagnetic) fields. They are the dynamic, functional organs of our EM body, which is a template that causes our physical bodies to materialize and manifest as it does. It is also through the EM field that our physical bodies are energized and are enabled to maintain a healthy state directly from God's consciousness."* (A chakra diagram with URL address to this article is in Appendix 3 on page 69).

Admittedly, some of the words used in the protocol keep many Christians away. We become afraid of doing something wrong or "un-Christian" and want to steer clear of anything that would give the enemy of our soul a foothold or a stronghold.

Fear has a way of holding us back...it's paralyzing. So, this began my journey to understand, to seek God for wisdom and revelation and to modify the emotional release language with *His* words.

I know essential oils work. I believe they and you are God's idea! He spoke every plant into existence and breathed life into you. And He has given you a heart to know Him. *"I will give them a heart to know me, that I am the LORD. They will be my people, and I will be their God, for they will return to me with all their heart."* Jeremiah 24:7. There is only one who wants to keep you afraid and in bondage. His plan for you is to steal, kill and destroy. But Jesus said, *"I have come that they may have life and have it to the full."* John 10:10. Life, **abundant life**...is what God wants for you. **This is why I wrote *Reboot*! I want EVERYONE to experience emotional freedom and the abundant life!!** *"Praise be to the God and Father of our Lord Jesus Christ, the Father of compassion and the God of all comfort, who comforts us in all our troubles, so that we can comfort those in any trouble with the comfort we ourselves receive from God. For just as we share abundantly in the sufferings of Christ, so also our comfort abounds through Christ.* 2 Corinthians 1:3-5.

"It is for freedom that Christ has set us free." Galatians 5:1a. Until the age of 40, most of my life was lived in bondage to fear. I was afraid of people. I was afraid of being rejected. I was afraid of disappointing people; I was afraid of failing. Bottom line, I was afraid. Through pastoral counsel at the age of 40, I was powerfully delivered from a spirit of fear and gloriously experienced what 1 John 4:18 says...*"perfect love casts out all fear."* I was so deceived I didn't even know I was living a life of fear, but I definitely knew when I wasn't! And finally, the longing for my Father was completely satisfied. *The Spirit you received does not make you slaves, so that you live in fear again; rather, the Spirit you received brought about your adoption to sonship. And by him we cry, 'Abba, Father.'"* Romans 8:15.

Emotions - What are They?

Emotions, often called feelings, include experiences such as love, hate, anger, trust, joy, discouraged, panic, calm, fear, and grief. Emotions are related to, but differ from, mood. Emotions are specific reactions to an event that is usually of short duration. Mood is a more general feeling such as happiness, sadness, frustration, contentment, or anxiety that lasts for a longer time.

Although everyone experiences emotions, scientists do not all agree on what emotions are or how they should be measured or studied. Emotions are complex and have both physical and mental components. Generally, researchers agree that emotions have the following parts: subjective feelings, physiological (body) responses, and expressive behavior.

The component of emotions that scientists call subjective feelings refers to the way each individual person experiences feelings, and this component is the most difficult to describe or measure. Subjective feelings cannot be observed; instead, the person experiencing the emotion must describe it to others, and each person's description and interpretation of a feeling may be slightly different. For example, two people falling in love will not experience or describe their feeling in the same ways.

Physiological responses are the easiest part of emotion to measure because scientists have developed special tools to measure them. A pounding heart, sweating, blood rushing to the face, or the release of **adrenaline*** in response to a situation that creates intense emotion can all be measured with scientific accuracy. People have very similar internal responses to the same emotion. For example, regardless of age, race, or gender, when people are under stress, their bodies release adrenaline; this hormone helps prepare the body to either run away or fight, which is called the "fight or flight" reaction. Although the psychological part of emotions may be different for each feeling, several different emotions can produce the same physical reaction.

Expressive behavior is the outward sign that an emotion is being experienced. Outward signs of emotions can include fainting, a flushed face, muscle tensing, facial expressions, tone of voice, rapid breathing, restlessness, or other body language. The outward expression of an emotion gives other people clues to what someone is experiencing and helps to regulate social interactions.

*adrenaline (a-DREN-a-lin), also called epinephrine, (ep-e-NEF-rin), is a hormone, or chemical messenger, that is released in response to fear, anger, panic, and other emotions. It readies the body to respond to the threat by increasing heart rate, breathing rate, and blood flow to the arms and legs. These and other effects prepare the body to run away or fight. [Fight or Flight]. Read more: http://www.humanillnesses.com/Behavioral-Health-Br-Fe/Emotions.html#ixzz4nx8ziAtL

The Limbic System

Have you ever smelled something, and it immediately reminded you of someone, a time in your life or a place? You may have even spontaneously cried or laughed depending on whether the memory was happy, sad, or traumatic. This reaction is your limbic system at work (See diagram in Appendix 1). When we inhale the aroma of something like baked goods, fried food, grass or an essential oil, the odor molecules travel through the nose where they register with nerves in the olfactory membranes in the nose lining. The odor molecules stimulate this lining of nerve cells and trigger electrical impulses to the olfactory bulb in the brain. The olfactory bulb then transmits the impulses to the amygdala - where emotional memories are stored - and to other parts of the limbic system of the brain. The unique structure of the molecules of essential oils can directly stimulate the hypothalamus and limbic lobe of the brain. Inhaling essential oils may alleviate stress and emotional trauma as well as increase the production of thyroid and growth hormones.

The amygdala (where emotional memories are stored) plays a major role in the storage and release of emotional trauma. Our sense of smell is directly linked to emotional states and behaviors, even if they have been stored since childhood. Our sense of smell, one of the five senses, is the ONLY way to stimulate the amygdala. **The amygdala does not respond to words said or words heard. This is why the use of essential oils is so therapeutic to the release of stored emotions. Essential oils enable us to access stored or forgotten memories and/or suppressed emotions. This allows us to acknowledge, integrate or release them.** If we don't, these memories and suppressed emotions can cause *dis-ease* in our bodies such as feeling blue or feeling afraid. Essential oils combined with prayer and seeking the Holy Spirit (and other modalities such as massage) can have a healing effect on our mind, emotions, and body, especially when we incorporate them into our daily practice.

Broken Record

You might be asking, "Really? Essential oils can help my emotions?" Yes! Let me explain using the example of vinyl record. I know, I'm dating myself now because many of you reading this may have never even played that black, vinyl disc and quite possibly have never seen one. If that, is you, think of a CD or DVD instead. Back in my day, we would put a flat, black, vinyl disc, called a record (reh-kurd) on the record player. You had to carefully handle the vinyl by the edges because it was somewhat soft and could easily scratch. Even fingerprints could affect the proper playing of a record. Normally, a tiny needle would glide across the light, circular lines in the vinyl and each song would

play as intended. If the vinyl was scratched, the song would play until the needle met the scratch. If the scratch was minor, the needle may just skip over it or an unintended scratchy sound would play with the music. But if the scratch was severe, it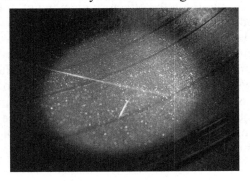

would bounce the needle back to a previous groove replaying the same part of the song repeatedly. At some point, you would become aware that a portion of the song was being continually repeated. We would say the record is "stuck" wo you would have to deliberately and gently nudge the needle to help it get past the scratch without scratching it more. A scratched record would sound like this: *"Amazing grace, how sweet the sound, that saved a wre, Amazing grace, how sweet the sound, that saved a wre, Amazing grace, how sweet the sound, that saved a wre,"* ...you get the idea. It is possible that cleaning the record with a soft cloth would remove or clean the scratch well enough that the record would play the song as it was intended.

So, what does a record or a scratched record have to do with an emotional release? Think of that record with its evenly spaced lines as your brain recording, organizing, and storing everything

 you have ever experienced. Good experiences would be like the normal, melodious lines in a record and bad or traumatic experiences would be like scratches on the vinyl. As you go about your life, there are times; days, months and even years that your thoughts fall into that scratched groove and it "gets stuck" and without even realizing it, keeps replaying a memory or emotion over and over and over. Many times, we go through life without realizing that our thoughts and our decisions are being influenced by those memories and emotions in "scratched-record" fashion. People may even describe you as being touchy or sounding like a "broken record". Or you might even think of yourself as feeling stuck. Now think of the molecules of essential oils as the deliberate, gentle nudge or soft, buffing cloth, that gently removes or releases that memory or emotion, so you can live the life you were intended to; a positive, healthy, happy, and abundant life. **It's like remembering the original you.**

Your Operating System

Another way to look at releasing emotions with **Reboot** is to think about the function of a computer. When you purchase a new computer, it comes pre-installed with an operating system and programs. Over time and use, it may become bogged down due to random-access memory (RAM) issues, a full hard drive, or a computer virus. If you are fixing the RAM issue, you may need to clear the cache. If you are fixing a full hard drive, you may need to delete documents, pictures, or videos to free up space. If you are fixing a virus, installing, and running an antivirus software

program can detect and eliminate a virus. Sometimes a soft boot; simultaneously pressing control + alt + delete will work. All of these "fixes" are like the actions of essential oils on our emotions.

When each of us were created in the secret place, it was to a specific code called DNA, which causes us to look, sound and act as we do (our pre-installed, default operating system). *"I praise you because I am fearfully and wonderfully made; your works are wonderful; I know that full well."* Psalm 139:14. As we grow, mature and experience life on earth as human beings, we go through hard times; disappointment, loss, sickness, abuse, trauma, betrayal, and sadness. These difficulties cause us to store emotions in our cellular memory which leave "soul wounds" that bog us down much like a RAM issue or an overloaded hard drive. *"What a wretched man I am! Who will rescue me from this body that is subject to death?" Romans 7:24.* Using the essential oils in **Reboot** is like scanning your "operating system" for viruses (recurring, pervasive thoughts, faulty and limiting beliefs, stored, traumatic memories) and putting them in quarantine until restarting your computer eliminates them. Using essential oils for emotional release is like pressing Control + Alt + Delete. This is an intentional and soft **Reboot**. *"Create in me a clean heart, O God, and renew a right spirit in me."* Psalm 51:10. This is the power of essential oils; tiny molecules that God spoke into existence so that we can recognize and release that which isn't serving us or Him well.

Then God said, *"Let the land produce vegetation: seed-bearing plants and trees on the land that bear fruit with seed in it, according to their various kinds." And it was so. The land produced vegetation: plants bearing seed according to their kinds and trees bearing fruit with seed in it according to their kinds. And God saw that it was good. And there was evening, and there was morning—the third day."* Genesis 1:11-13. God blessed them and said to them, *"Then God said, "Let us make mankind in our image, in our likeness, so that they may rule over the fish in the sea and the birds in the sky, over the livestock and all the wild animals, and over all the creatures that move along the ground." So, God created mankind in his own image, in the image of God he created them; male and female he created them. Be fruitful and increase in number; fill the earth and subdue it. Rule over the fish in the sea and the birds in the sky and over every living creature that moves on the ground." Then God said, "I give you every seed-bearing plant on the face of the whole earth and every tree that has fruit with seed in it. They will be yours for food. And to all the beasts of the earth and all the birds in the sky and all the creatures that move along the ground—everything that has the breath of life in it—I give every green plant for food." And it was so."* Genesis 1:26-31. Our good God, our Father in heaven, created all the plants on the *third* day and He created man on the *sixth* day. Therefore, He provided everything we needed **before** we ever needed them. Yes! GOD IS THAT GOOD!

What are Essential Oils?

In her book, ***Therapeutic Blending with Essential Oil,*** Rebecca Park Totila says: "Essential oils are a fragrant, vital fluid distilled from flowers, shrubs, leaves, trees, roots, and seeds. Because they are necessary for the life of a plant and play a vital role in the biological process of the vegetation these substances are called *essential* because they carry the lifeblood, intelligence and vibrational energy that endow them with the healing power to sustain their own life--and help people [physically, mentally, emotionally] who use them." (Brackets mine). Essential oils are often referred to as the "life-blood" of the plant.

Did you know that essential oils contain around 100 to 300 natural compounds and even thousands of other trace compounds that scientists have not yet identified? This is exactly what makes the specific chemistry of an individual essential oil nearly impossible to replicate in a laboratory. Climate conditions, exposure to pollutants, processes used to extract essential oil from a plant can affect and influence an essential oils aroma and its therapeutic powers.

Phenols, Sesquiterpenes and Monoterpenes

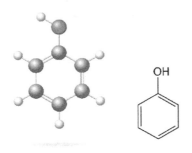

Essential oil compounds could be categorized into two major chemical groups; hydrocarbons and oxygenated compounds. Hydrocarbons are made up of terpenes; monoterpenes, sesquiterpenes, diterpenes, triterpenes and oxygenated compounds consist of esters, aldehydes, ketones, alcohols, phenols, and oxides. Let's take a brief look at the actions of phenols (P), sesquiterpenes (S) and monoterpenes (M) and the role they play at cell receptor sites.

Cell Receptor Sites

What are cell receptor sites? Every cell in your body has thousands of locations on its surface that serve as "mini" sense organs, called receptor sites. These receptor sites are proteins that are on the surface of each cell. They act as little receivers (or ears) that listen to the messages of the chemical messenger molecules as they float in the intercellular fluid surrounding every cell. Another way to think of this is to consider each receptor site as a lock that is capable of receiving particular types of chemical messenger keys, called ligands. I like to think of cell receptor sites as a lock and a key system.

This is easiest to understand if we think of the front door of our home. Most homes, if not all, have a doorknob that has a lock. Each lock has a specific key or code that will unlock the door and allow you to enter. If you don't have the correct key or correct code, the lock will not open and essentially you are locked out. Sometimes the lock gets "gunked up" or malfunctions and you are unable to get the key in. You may even need to repair the lock. So, we look for an outside source, like a can of WD40 (think phenolic essential oil) and spray it into the lock to remove the gunk. Other times we need to have the lock re-keyed and then have new keys made or choose a new code. Get it? This is a considerably basic way of understanding and explaining the job of phenols, sesquiterpenes and monoterpenes in essential oils. Essential oils may contain all three compounds but are predominantly one type. Essential oils that contain compounds that are heavily phenolic will go to cell receptor sites and *scrub* it clean. Essential oils that contain compounds that are primarily high in sesquiterpenes and are found in most essential oils, *deprogram* cell receptor sites, or remove miswritten or bad information. Essential oils primarily high in monoterpenes are known as *reprogrammers* or write good information. I remember it with this acronym: **PSM: P**henols – Scrub, **S**esquiterpenes – Deprogram, **M**onoterpenes – Reprogram

For a list of essential oils that are high in each of the categories, see Appendix 2. I encourage you to do further research and learn more about the chemistry of essential oils and highly recommend another book by David Stewart, Ph.D., D.N.M, ***The Chemistry of Essential Oils Made Simple***. Purchase at the *Center for Aromatherapy Research and Education* here: www.raindroptraining.com.

Is *Reboot* right for you?

One question could sum it up...are you human? Any living, breathing human being who has faced hard situations or adversities in life will benefit from ***Reboot***. Look over the list below and write "yes" or place a check mark on the line if you have experienced any of these feelings or situations.

_____ I feel anger or hate most of the time

_____ I am smiling on the outside, but crying on the inside

_____ I often feel lonely even in large crowds

_____ I have experienced life-altering events such as betrayal, divorce or the death of a child, sibling, or spouse

_____ I feel stuck

_____ I am in a cycle of self-abuse/self-sabotage/self-harm

_____ I feel insignificant

_____ I often wonder if there is more to life

_____ I have been physically abused

_____ I have been sexually abused

_____ I have been mentally abused

_____ I have experienced religious abuse

_____ I have had a debilitating accident

_____ I have experienced traumatic events that altered the course of my life.

_____ I always seem to "miss the mark"

_____ I am/have been addicted to substances (alcohol or drugs)

_____ I lack joy in daily living

_____ I am searching for purpose and meaning in my life

_____ My self-talk is negative

_____ People say I am hard on myself

_____ I have dis-ease in my body

_____ I am an adult but feel like a child emotionally

_____ I have contemplated suicide

_____ My spiritual growth is stagnated

_____ I can't seem to get past my past

_____ Relationships are difficult

_____ I stuff my emotions

_____ I feel hopeless, like I am at the end of my rope

_____ I am an emotional eater

_____ I feel unworthy of love

_____ I have been rejected or abandoned

_____ I have exhausted all other resources for emotional freedom

_____ I have been described as being an overly sensitive person

_____ People tell me they have to "walk on eggshells" around me

_____ I have occasional, short periods of explosive anger

_____ I desire to make healthy choices for myself, my children, and future generations.

_____ I am open to an emotional release protocol.

This is not an exhaustive list by any means, but if you answered yes to any of these questions, then **Reboot** may be right for you. Pray, ask God to make it clear to you if **Reboot** is right for you and trust His plan for your life. *(Note: I strongly encourage and know that there are many benefits of seeking pastoral and/or professional help when needed. Asking for help is a step in the right direction, not a weakness.)*

"For I know the plans I have for you," declares the Lord, *"plans to prosper you and not to harm you, plans to give you hope and a future."* Jeremiah 29:11

BEFORE You Begin *Reboot*

Please consider these guidelines before beginning and to be best prepared for *Reboot*:

1. Decide if you are going to do the protocol alone, with a spouse, a close friend, a retreat group, or as an essential oils class. **In most states, there are laws requiring a license to touch. In class settings, allowing individuals to place the oils on themselves is preferred.**

2. In the case of a small or large group, each participant must be instructed to hold a safe, judgment-free space for all participants.

3. Shower/bathe just prior to *Reboot* so you can leave the oils on your body for at least 12 hours.

4. Allow at least ninety minutes of uninterrupted time for *Reboot*, prayer, and pampering.

5. Dress in comfortable, loose-fitting clothing.

6. Use the restroom before beginning so you can complete *Reboot* without interruption.

7. Silence all cell phones or place them in another room.

8. Have a pillow and a blanket so you can do most of the protocol laying down. If doing *Reboot* alone, you can do in a bedroom while lying on the bed.

9. The room should be dimly lit, a comfortable temperature and quiet. Some people prefer soft music (without words) playing in the background, but this can be distracting to other participants if in a group.

10. Arrange each of the 14 oils used in *Reboot* in order of their use: Valor, Harmony, Sacred Frankincense, 3 Wise Men, Release, Believe, Inner Child, Forgiveness, Grounding, Hope, Joy, Present Time, SARA, White Angelica.

11. IMPORTANT: Be sure to have a bottle of Young Living's V-6 Oil (or another carrier oil like olive or coconut oil) nearby just in case you or any participant(s) get essential oils in or near their eyes or has any skin sensitivity to the essential oils.

12. Keep a glass of water, a Bible, and a pen within reach.

13. If doing *Reboot* in a group, designate a facilitator who will read the reawaken step and distribute the essential oil blends to each participant. They will also read the realign and reaffirm steps.

14. If at any time you or a participant feels uncomfortable, stop *Reboot* briefly and drink water. Pray. Ask the Holy Spirit if there is anything that is preventing you from going forward. Begin again and if any issues remain, stop. Try again in a few days.

15. In the Reflect portion, date, and record any thoughts, memories, emotions, visions, revelations, or scriptures that are brought to your mind as you use each oil. If you experience emotional release such as crying or heavy sighing, make a note in the space provided.

16. Consider asking a trusted friend or family member to pray for you or your group during the entire *Reboot*.

17. Pray, ask God to guide you and to speak to you through the power of His Holy Spirit.

Understanding "RE"

Miriam-Webster defines "RE" as again, anew, retell [tell again]. (Brackets mine). We need to be reminded (mind again) or reassured (assured again) of the truth often. *"Where there is no vision, my people perish."* Proverbs 29:18.

Reboot - Boot again   **Reawaken - Awaken again**
Realign - Align again   **Reaffirm - Affirm again**

Reboot for emotional release may be experienced several ways. For maximum results, consider the time, setting and number of participants who are going to *Reboot*. **Reawaken** by applying all 14 oils as directed and then in any order and in any combination follow with Realign, Reaffirm, and/or Reflect. For example:

Reawaken = 30 minutes,

Reawaken + Realign (or Reaffirm) = 60 minutes

Reawaken + Realign + Reaffirm = 90 minutes

Reawaken + Realign + Reaffirm + Reflect - 120 minutes

Note: Reawaken is the only <u>required</u> step and must be completed <u>before</u> Realign, Reaffirm and/or Reflect.

1. **REAWAKEN** - (30 minutes) **The REAWAKEN step is required.** It is the application of all fourteen essential oils to specific locations on the body and slowly and deeply inhaling the aroma of each oil. The aroma of the essential oils reaches the limbic system, raises your vibrational energy, and helps you remember and release emotions. Reawaken is great for anyone, anytime. It is the perfect choice for individuals and small or large essential oil retreats and classes.

2. **REALIGN** - (30 minutes) The REALIGN step includes meditating on Biblical truth after you have applied each of the *Reboot* oils. Realign is a great choice for personal

development, Sabbath, couple's prayer time, Bible study groups, essential oil classes, spiritual retreats, church board retreats, and spiritual counseling. See also the Alternative Daily Reboot Method on the next page.

3. **REAFFIRM** - (30 minutes) The REAFFIRM step focuses on being intentional as you think, speak, and feel each affirmation for each of the fourteen oils in *Reboot*. Touch your forehead as you *think* each affirmation (mind). Touch your mouth as you audibly *speak* each affirmation (body). Touch your heart as you *feel* each affirmation (spirit) giving extra time to feel each affirmation.

   Another way to use the affirmations is to bring into alignment the Holy Trinity. I think of God the Father as I touch my head/mind, Jesus the Son as I touch my mouth and the Holy Spirit as I touch my heart. It is okay to repeat the affirmations several times. Adding the *reaffirm* section is a great choice for personal development, small classes, business-building, team enrichment, business or board retreats and meetings.

4. **REFLECT** - (30 minutes) The Reflect step is for listening to your heart. Time to listen and just BE. Write in the space provided or in a personal journal any thoughts or memories that surface, emotions released, visions, revelations, affirmations, scriptures or how the Holy Spirit is speaking. *"As water reflects the face, so one's life reflects the heart."* Proverbs 27:19

Alternative DAILY *Reboot* Method

Each morning upon waking, do the Reawaken step with just one *Reboot* oil in the order given. For example, on day one, use Valor, on day two, use Harmony, on day three, Sacred Frankincense and so on until you have used all fourteen oils in *Reboot*. Meditate on the scriptures and/or affirmations as your time allows. In as little as 5 minutes a day, you will have completed *Reboot* and gently released emotions in two weeks. Repeat once a month or as often as you wish. Hint: Starting on the first of each month with the first oil will help you stay on track. Keep all *Reboot* oils on your nightstand so you can *Reboot* each day before you get out of bed. Lamentations 3:22-23 – "B*ecause of the Lord's great love we are not consumed, for his compassions never fail. They are new every morning; great is your faithfulness.*"

What to Expect DURING *Reboot*

1. Strong, therapeutic, pleasant aromas from each of the essential oils.
2. God's love and peace.
3. No judgment. (*"There is no condemnation for those in Christ Jesus."* Romans 8:1).
4. Emotional release which may manifest as sighing, crying, sobbing or headache.
5. Repressed or forgotten memories coming to the surface or into your awareness.
6. Visions. Revelations. Freedom.
7. Relaxation. Take your time.
8. Expect emotional release to occur during or after you have completed *Reboot* or not at all. That's ok. We are all different and respond differently to essential oils. There is nothing wrong with you if you do not experience emotional release immediately. Be assured that the essential oils are still working and *Reboot* again.
9. **It is worth repeating.... if there are issues that manifest that need further, deeper work, getting pastoral and/or professional support is encouraged!**

Anosmia

Through the years, I have encountered several people who have completely lost their sense of smell. This is known as acquired anosmia (an-OHZ-me-uh). Most anosmics may still benefit from aromatherapy. For example, if an anosmic smokes cigarettes, they do not have to be able to smell the cigarette smoke to feel the effects of the nicotine. In the same way, anosmics may not have to smell an essential oil to feel the effects of the unique constituents in essential oils.

In their commitment to helping people live life to its fullest through essential oils, Young Living has partnered with Monell Chemical Senses Center, the only independent, non-profit scientific institute dedicated to basic research on taste and smell. Young Living provides essential oils and financial support for smell training to help people regain their sense of smell.

Pray. *"Search me, God, and know my heart; test me and know my anxious thoughts. See if there is any offensive way in me and lead me in the way everlasting."* Psalm 139:23-24.

VALOR

Deuteronomy 31:6 - *"Be strong and courageous. Do not be afraid or terrified because of them, for the Lord your God goes with you; he will never leave you nor forsake you."*

REAWAKEN with Young Living's **Valor**, the first oil used in **Reboot**. **Valor** is a blend of essential oils containing the following: Black Spruce, Camphor Wood, Blue Tansy, Frankincense and Geranium. Item #3430 - 5 ml bottle - $41.25 / $54.28 Cost per drop: $0.55 / $0.72

Apply 4 – 6 drops of **Valor** to the palm of your non-dominant hand and place your hands together to get the oils on both hands. Then apply to the bottoms of the feet. Place your right palm to the bottom of your right foot and place your left palm to apply to the bottom of the left foot. If this is difficult or awkward, place 2 drops of Valor on your wrist and place your wrists together. Close your eyes. Focus on your feet (or wrists) until you feel a simultaneous pulse, energy, or a wave-like sensation in each foot/wrist. **Valor** balances the electrical energy in your body. **Valor** may help you overcome fear and opposition. Therefore, we start **Reboot** with **Valor**. **Valor** may give you courage, confidence and increase your self-esteem. Through your nose, inhale **Valor** deeply and slowly 5 – 10 times.

REALIGN with God's word by meditating on the following scriptures as **Valor** is used:

1. Psalm 55:18 - *"He rescues me unharmed from the battle waged against me, even though many oppose me."*
2. Isaiah 40:29 - *"He gives strength to the weary and increases the power of the weak."*
3. Isaiah 41:10 - *"So do not fear, for I am with you; do not be dismayed, for I am your God. I will strengthen you and help you; I will uphold you with my righteous right hand."*
4. Romans 8:31 - *"What, then, shall we say in response to these things? If God is for us, who can be against us?"*
5. Romans 8:37 - *"No, in all these things we are more than conquerors through Him who loved us."*

REAFFIRM: I am _____

(Put your full, given name here)
As you breathe **Valor** from your hands, think, say, and feel the following affirmations: *I am balanced. I am confident. I am courageous. I am brave. I am strong. I am victorious.*

REFLECT: Record your own scriptures, thoughts, emotions, or prayers here as the Holy Spirit leads you.

Date: _____

_____
_____
_____
_____
_____

Date: _____

_____
_____
_____
_____
_____

Date: _____

_____
_____
_____
_____
_____

Date: _____

_____
_____
_____
_____
_____

"You gain strength, courage and confidence by every experience in which you stop to look fear in the face." **Eleanor Roosevelt**

HARMONY

Psalm 133:1 - *"How good and pleasant it is when God's people live together in unity."*

REAWAKEN with Young Living's **Harmony**, the second oil used in *Reboot*. **Harmony** is a blend of essential oils containing the following: Sacred Sandalwood, Lavender, Ylang Ylang, Frankincense, Orange, Angelica, Geranium, Hyssop, Spanish sage, Black spruce, Coriander, Bergamot, Lemon, Jasmine, Roman chamomile, Palmarosa, and Rose.
Item #3351 - 15 ml bottle - $74.50 / $98.03
Cost per drop: $0.30 / $0.40

Apply 1-2 drops of **Harmony** to your non-dominant hand. With your pointer and middle finger, activate the oil three times in a clockwise motion. Apply **Harmony** with these two fingers to your body's energy centers; Crown, Between the eyes, Throat, Heart, Solar Plexus, Sacral and Root (see Energy Center Diagram in Appendix 3). **Harmony** may reduce stress and create a general overall sense of well-being. Through your nose, inhale **Harmony** deeply and slowly 5 – 10 times.

REALIGN with God's word by meditating on the following scriptures as **Harmony** is used:

1. Psalm 122:8 - *"For the sake of my family and friends, I will say, 'Peace be within you.'"*
2. Matthew 22:37-40 - *"Love the Lord your God with all your heart and with all your soul and with all your mind. This is the first and greatest commandment. And the second is like it, 'Love your neighbor as yourself.'"*
3. Philippians 4:8-9 - *"Finally, brothers and sisters, whatever is true, whatever is noble, whatever is right, whatever is pure, whatever is lovely, whatever is admirable—if anything is excellent or praiseworthy—think about such things. Whatever you have learned or received or heard from me, or seen in me—put it into practice. And the God of peace will be with you."*

REAFFIRM: I am _____
(Put your full, given name here)
As you breathe **Harmony** from your hands, think, say, and feel the following affirmations: *I am harmonious. I am completely balanced. I am peaceful. I belong.*

REFLECT: Record your own scriptures, thoughts, emotions, or prayers here as the Holy Spirit leads you.

Date: _____

_____
_____
_____
_____
_____

Date: _____

_____
_____
_____
_____
_____

Date: _____

_____
_____
_____
_____
_____

Date: _____

_____
_____
_____
_____
_____

"My belief is that God created human beings and therefore he knows about every aspect of the human body. So, if I want to fix it, I just need to stay in harmony with Him." **Ben Carson**

SACRED FRANKINCENSE

Mark 4:39 - "He got up, rebuked the wind and said to the waves, "Quiet! Be still!" Then the wind died down and it was completely calm."

<u>REAWAKEN</u> with Young Living's **Sacred Frankincense,** the third oil in Reboot. **Sacred Frankincense** is a single oil. It only contains 100% pure **Sacred Frankincense**.
Item #3550 - 5 ml bottle - $45.25 / $59.94
Cost per drop $0.60 / $0.80
Item #3552 - 15 ml bottle - $96.25 / $126.64
Cost per drop $0.39 / $0.51

Apply 1-2 drops of **Sacred Frankincense** to your non-dominant hand. With your pointer and middle finger, activate the oil three times in a clockwise motion. Apply **Sacred Frankincense** with these two fingers to the temples, back of the neck, top of the head and over your heart. **Sacred Frankincense** may help regulate emotions especially during times of stress, loss, or trauma. **Sacred Frankincense** is very calming and allows one to go deeper spiritually. Through your nose, inhale **Sacred Frankincense** deeply and slowly 5 – 10 times.

<u>REALIGN</u> with God's word by meditating on the following scriptures as **Sacred Frankincense** is used:

1. Matthew 2:11 - *"On coming to the house, they saw the child with his mother Mary, and they bowed down and worshiped him. Then they opened their treasures and presented him with gifts of gold, frankincense and myrrh."*
2. John 16:13 - *"But when he, the Spirit of truth, comes, he will guide you into all the truth. He will not speak on his own; he will speak only what he hears, and he will tell you what is yet to come."*
3. Hebrews 6:19-20a - *"We have this hope as an anchor for the soul, firm and secure. It enters the inner sanctuary behind the curtain, where our forerunner, Jesus, has entered on our behalf."*

REAFFIRM: I am _____
(Put your full, given name here)

As you breathe **Sacred Frankincense** from your hands, think, say, and feel the following affirmations: *I am sacred. I am body. I am soul. I am spirit. I am whole. I am worthy.*

REFLECT: Record your own scriptures, thoughts, emotions, or prayers here as the Holy Spirit leads you.

Date: _____
_____
_____
_____
_____
_____

Date: _____
_____
_____
_____
_____
_____

Date: _____
_____
_____
_____
_____
_____

Date: _____
_____
_____
_____
_____
_____

"Your own mind is a sacred enclosure into which nothing harmful can enter except by your permission." Arnold Bennett

3 WISE MEN

Proverbs 3:7-8 - *"Do not be wise in your own eyes, fear the Lord and shun evil. This will bring health to your body and nourishment to your bones."*

REAWAKEN with Young Living's **3 Wise Men**, the fourth oil in *Reboot.*
3 Wise Men is a blend of essential oils containing the following: Sweet Almond Oil, Royal Hawaiian Sandalwood, Juniper, Frankincense, Black Spruce and Myrrh.
Item #3426 - 15 ml bottle, $94.00 / $123.68
Cost per drop: $0.38 / $0.50

Apply 1-2 drops of **3 Wise Men** to the non-dominant hand. With your pointer and middle finger, activate the oil 3 times in a clockwise motion. Apply **3 Wise Men** to the crown of the head in a clockwise circular motion. **3 Wise Men** may open the crown energy center and stimulate the pineal gland to release emotions and deep-seated trauma. It brings a sense of grounding and uplifting through memory recall. It may also help keep negative energy and emotions from reattaching to the body. Smell **3 Wise Men** deeply and slowly 5 – 10 times.

REALIGN with God's word by meditating on the following scriptures as **3 Wise Men** is used:

1. Proverbs 3:21-23 - *"My son, do not let wisdom and understanding out of your sight, preserve sound judgment and discretion; they will be life for you, an ornament to grace your neck. Then you will go on your way in safety, and your foot will not stumble."*
2. Psalm 119:105 - *"Your word is a lamp unto my feet and a light unto my path."*
3. James 1:5 - *"If any of you lacks wisdom, you should ask God, who gives generously to all without finding fault, and it will be given to you."*

REAFFIRM: I am _____
(Put your full, given name here)

As you breathe **3 Wise Men** from your hands, think, say, and feel the following affirmations: *I am wise. I am grounded. I am uplifted. I am positive. My words are wise, trustworthy, and true.*

REFLECT: Record your own scriptures, thoughts, emotions, or prayers here as the Holy Spirit leads you.

Date: _____

_____
_____
_____
_____
_____

Date: _____

_____
_____
_____
_____
_____

Date: _____

_____
_____
_____
_____
_____

Date: _____

_____
_____
_____
_____
_____
_____

God grant me the serenity. to accept the things, I cannot change; courage to change the things I can; and wisdom to know the difference."
The Serenity Prayer

RELEASE

Ephesians 4:31 - *"Get rid of all bitterness, rage and anger, brawling and slander, along with every form of malice."*

REAWAKEN with Young Living's **Release**, the fifth oil in *Reboot*. **Release** is a blend of essential oils containing the following: Ylang-Ylang, Olive, Lavindin, Geranium, Royal Hawaiian Sandalwood, Grapefruit, Tangerine, Spearmint, Lemon, Blue Cypress, Davana, Lime, Ocotea, Jasmine, Matricaria, and Blue Tansy and Rose.
Item #3408 - 15 ml bottle - $40.75 / $53.62
Cost per drop: $0.16 / $0.21

Apply 1 – 2 drops of **Release** to your non-dominant hand. With your pointer and middle finger, activate the oil three times in a clockwise motion. Apply **Release** over your liver area (right side, just under your ribs). **Release** may help enhance the release of memory trauma from the cells of the liver, where hate and anger are stored. It may also help you let go of negative emotions so that progress is more efficient and effective. Through your nose, inhale **Release** deeply and slowly 5 – 10 times.

REALIGN with God's word by meditating on the following scriptures as **Release** is used:

1. Psalm 25:15 - *"My eyes are ever on the Lord, for only he will release my feet from the snare."*
2. Romans 7:6 - *"But now by dying to what once bound us, we have been released from the law so that we serve in the new way of the Spirit, and not in the old way of the written code.*
3. Romans 12:19 - *"Do not take revenge, my dear friends, but leave room for God's wrath, for it is written: "It is mine to avenge; I will repay," says the Lord."*
4. James 1:19 -20- *"My dear brothers and sisters, take note of this: Everyone should be quick to listen, slow to speak and slow to become angry, because human anger does not produce the righteousness that God desires."*

REAFFIRM: I am _____
(Put your full, given name here)

As you breathe **Release** from your hands, think, say, and feel the following affirmations: *I release all that does not serve me well. I choose to release hate and anger. I release.*

REFLECT: Record your own scriptures, thoughts, emotions, or prayers here as the Holy Spirit leads you.

Date: _____
_____
_____
_____
_____
_____

Date: _____
_____
_____
_____
_____
_____
_____

Date: _____
_____
_____
_____
_____
_____
_____

Date: _____
_____
_____
_____
_____
_____

"Those things we stuff, try so hard to ignore, they are the very things begging for release --- the things that hold the promise of hope, the flame of freedom."
JoAnn Fore

BELIEVE

Matthew 21:22 - *"If you believe, you will receive whatever you ask for in prayer."*

<u>**REAWAKEN**</u> with Young Living's **Believe**, the sixth oil in ***Reboot.*** (The EODR lists Idaho Balsam Fir in their guide for the sixth oil. I chose to use Believe, which lists IBF as the first oil in the blend). **Believe** is a blend of essential oils containing the following: Balsam Canada, Coriander, Bergamot, Frankincense, Idaho Blue Spruce, Ylang Ylang, and Geranium.
Item #4661 - 15 ml bottle - $40.00 / $52.63
Cost per drop: $0.16 / $0.21

Apply 1 – 2 drops of **Believe** to your non-dominant hand. With your pointer and middle finger, activate the oil three times in a clockwise motion. Apply **Believe** over the heart, on the wrists and on the forehead, temples, and neck. **Believe** may help you release emotional blocks and find strength, so you can reach your full, unlimited potential. Believe may also help you feel balanced, uplifted and calm. Through your nose, inhale **Believe** deeply and slowly 5 – 10 times.

<u>**REALIGN**</u> with God's word by meditating on the following scriptures as **Believe** is used:

1. Psalm 3:3 - *"But you, Lord, are a shield around me, my glory, the One who lifts my head high."*
2. Psalm 18:32 - *"It is God who arms me with strength and keeps my way secure."*
3. Mark 9:23 - *"'If you can?' said Jesus. 'Everything is possible for one who believes'".*
4. Mark 11:24 - *"Therefore I tell you, whatever you ask for in prayer,* believe *that you have received it, and it will be yours."*
5. James 1:6 - *"But when you ask, you must believe and not doubt, because the one who doubts is like a wave of the sea, blown and tossed by the wind."*

REAFFIRM: I am _____
(Put your full, given name here)

As you breathe **Believe** from your hands, think, say, and feel the following affirmations: *I am sure. I believe. I am believable. I am my full potential.*

REFLECT: Record your own scriptures, thoughts, emotions, or prayers here as the Holy Spirit leads you.

Date: _____

_____
_____
_____
_____
_____

Date: _____

_____
_____
_____
_____
_____

Date: _____

_____
_____
_____
_____
_____

Date: _____

_____
_____
_____
_____
_____

"Beliefs are choices. First you choose your beliefs. Then your beliefs affect your choices." **Roy T. Bennett**

INNER CHILD

Matthew 19:14 - "Jesus said, "Let the little children come to me, and do not hinder them, for the kingdom of heaven belongs to such as these."

REAWAKEN with Young Living's **Inner Child**, the seventh essential oil in *Reboot*. **Inner Child** is a blend of essential oils containing the following: Orange, Tangerine, Ylang-Ylang, Royal Hawaiian Sandalwood, Jasmine, Lemongrass, Spruce, Bitter Orange, and Neroli.
Item #3360 - 5 ml bottle - $31.75 / $41.78
Cost per drop: $0.42 / $0.56

Apply 1-2 drops of **Inner Child** to your non-dominant hand. With your pointer and middle finger, activate the oil three times in a clockwise motion. Apply **Inner Child** first around and in your navel and then around your nose. **Inner Child** may stimulate your memory response and help you reconnect with your inner self, your own true identity. This is one of the first steps in achieving emotional balance. Through your nose, inhale **Inner Child** deeply and slowly 5 – 10 times.

REALIGN with God's word by meditating on the following scriptures as **Inner Child** is used:

1. Psalm 139:14 - *"I praise you because I am fearfully and wonderfully made; your works are wonderful; I know that full well."*
2. Matthew 18:2-3 - *"He called a little child to him and placed the child among them. And he said: "Truly I tell you, unless you change and become like little children, you will never enter the kingdom of heaven. Therefore, whoever takes the lowly position of this child is the greatest in the kingdom of heaven. And whoever welcomes one such child in my name welcomes me."*
3. 1 John 3:1 - *"See what great love the Father has lavished on us, that we should be called children of God! And that is what we are!"*

REAFFIRM: I am _____

(Put or say your full given name here)

As you breathe **Inner Child** from your hands, think, say, and feel the following affirmations**:** *I am fully connected to I Am. I remember me. I am a child of God.*

REFLECT: Record your own scriptures, thoughts, emotions, prayers here as the Holy Spirit leads you.

Date: _____

_____
_____
_____
_____
_____
_____

Date: _____

_____
_____
_____
_____
_____
_____

Date: _____

_____
_____
_____
_____
_____
_____

Date: _____

_____
_____
_____
_____
_____
_____

"I came to believe that my identity goes beyond the outer roles I play. It transcends the ego. I came to understand that there is an authentic 'I' within - an 'I Am,' or divine spark within the soul." **Sue Monk Kidd**

FORGIVENESS

Colossians 3:13 - *"Bear with each other and forgive one another if any of you has a grievance against someone. Forgive as the Lord forgave you."*

<u>**REAWAKEN**</u> with Young Living's **Forgiveness**, the eighth essential oil in *Reboot.* **Forgiveness** is a blend of essential oils containing the following: Sesame Seed Oil, Melissa, Geranium, Frankincense, Royal Hawaiian Sandalwood, Coriander, Angelica, Lavender, Bergamot, Lemon, Ylang-Ylang, Jasmine, Helichrysum, Roman Chamomile, Palmarosa, Rose
Item #3339 - 5 ml bottle - $56.25 / $74.01
Cost per drop: $0.75 / $0.99

Apply 1 – 2 drops of **Forgiveness** to your non-dominant hand. With your pointer and middle finger, activate the oils three times in a clockwise motion. Apply **Forgiveness** in and around the navel in a clockwise motion. **Forgiveness** may help you move past any barriers in life. It may bring you into a higher spiritual awareness of your needs and raise your frequency to a point where you feel compelled to forgive, forget, let go and go on with your life. Through your nose, inhale Forgiveness deeply and slowly 5 – 10 times.

<u>**REALIGN**</u> with God's word by meditating on the following scriptures as **Forgiveness** is used:

1. Psalm 32:1 - *"Blessed is the one whose transgressions are forgiven, whose sins are covered."*
2. Luke 5:20 - *"When Jesus saw their faith, he said, "Friend, your sins are forgiven."*
3. Acts 2:38 - *"Peter replied, "Repent and be baptized, every one of you, in the name of Jesus Christ for the forgiveness of your sins. And you will receive the gift of the Holy Spirit."*

On this step, ask the Holy Spirit to help you recall anyone you choose to forgive. Say quietly, "I forgive _____ (say the name of a person you CHOOSE to forgive…it may even be yourself).

REAFFIRM: I am _____

(Put your full, given name here)

As you breathe **Forgiveness** from your hands, think, say, and feel the following affirmations: *I am moving forward. I choose to forgive. I am forgiven. I am free. I am covered.*

REFLECT: Record your own scriptures, thoughts, emotions, or prayers here as the Holy Spirit leads you.

Date: _____
_____
_____
_____
_____
_____

Date: _____
_____
_____
_____
_____
_____

Date: _____
_____
_____
_____
_____
_____

Date: _____
_____
_____
_____
_____
_____

"He who cannot forgive breaks the bridge over which he himself must pass."
George Herbert

GROUNDING

Ephesians 3:16-19 - *"I pray that out of his glorious riches he may strengthen you with power through his Spirit in your inner being, so that Christ may dwell in your hearts through faith. And I pray that you, being rooted and established in love, may have power, together with all the Lord's holy people, to grasp how wide and long and high and deep is the love of Christ, and to know this love that surpasses knowledge—that you may be filled to the measure of all the fullness of God."*

<u>REAWAKEN</u> with Young Living's **Grounding**, the ninth essential oil in ***Reboot.*** **Grounding** is a blend of essential oils containing the following: White fir, Black Spruce, Ylang-Ylang, Pine, Cedarwood, Angelica, and Juniper.
Item #3348 - 5 ml bottle - $19.00 / $25.00
Cost per drop: $0.12 / $0.33

Apply 1 - 2 drops of **Grounding** to your non-dominant hand. With your pointer and middle finger, activate the oil three times in a clockwise motion. Apply **Grounding** to the brain stem, back of the neck and on your sternum (breastbone). **Grounding** may help you deal with the reality of your emotions in a peaceful way. Through your nose, inhale **Grounding** deeply and slowly 5 – 10 times.

<u>REALIGN</u> with God's word by meditating on the following scriptures as **Grounding** is used:

1. Isaiah 61:1-3 - *"The Spirit of the Sovereign LORD is on me because the LORD has anointed me to proclaim good news to the poor. He has sent me to bind up the brokenhearted, to proclaim freedom for the captives and release from darkness for the prisoners, to proclaim the year of the LORD's favor and the day of vengeance of our God, to comfort all who mourn, and provide for those who grieve in Zion—to bestow on them a crown of beauty instead of ashes, the oil of joy instead of mourning, and a garment of praise instead of a spirit of despair. They will be called **oaks of righteousness**, a planting of the LORD for the display of his splendor."*
2. Hebrews 6:19a – *"We have this hope as an anchor for the soul, firm and secure."*

REAFFIRM: I am _____
(Put your full, given name here)

As you breathe **Grounding** from your hands, think, say, and feel the following affirmations: *I am grounded. I am stable. I am calm.*

REFLECT: Record your own scriptures, thoughts, emotions, or prayers here as the Holy Spirit leads you.

Date: _____

_____
_____
_____
_____
_____
_____

Date: _____

_____
_____
_____
_____
_____
_____

Date: _____

_____
_____
_____
_____
_____
_____

Date: _____

_____
_____
_____
_____
_____
_____

"Flying starts from the ground. The more grounded you are, the higher you fly." **J.R. Rim**

HOPE

Proverbs 13:12 - *"Hope deferred makes the heart sick, but a longing fulfilled is a tree of life."*

REAWAKEN with Young Living's **Hope**, the tenth essential oil in *Reboot*. **Hope** is a blend of essential oils containing the following: Sweet Almond Oil, Melissa, Juniper, Myrrh, and Black Spruce.
Item # 3357 - 5 ml bottle - $61.00 / $80.26
Cost per drop: $0.81 / $1.07

Apply 1-2 drops of **Hope** to your non-dominant hand. With your pointer and middle finger, activate the oil three times in a clockwise motion. Apply **Hope** to the outer edge of both ears. **Hope** may help support the body physically and mentally. It may even help you overcome depression and restore hope for tomorrow. **Hope** may fill you with a sense of strength and grounding and may empower you to move forward with hope and achievement. Through your nose, inhale **Hope** deeply and slowly 5 – 10 times.

REALIGN with God's word by meditating on the following scriptures as **Hope** is being used:

1. Psalm 33:20 - *"We wait in hope for the Lord, he is our help and our shield."*
2. Psalm 146:5 - *"Blessed are those whose help is the God of Jacob; whose hope is in the Lord their God."*
3. Isaiah 40:30-31 - *"Even youths grow tired and weary, and young men stumble and fall; but those who hope in the Lord will renew their strength."*
4. Romans 5:3-5 - *"Not only so, but we also glory in our sufferings, because we know that suffering produces perseverance; perseverance, character; and character, hope. And hope does not put us to shame, because God's love has been poured out into our hearts through the Holy Spirit, who has been given to us."*

REAFFIRM: I am _____

(Put your full, given name here)

As you breathe **Hope** from your hands, think, think, say, and feel the following affirmations: *I am hopeful. I am restored. I welcome each new day. I have what I hope for now.*

REFLECT: Record your own scriptures, thoughts, emotions, or prayers here as the Holy Spirit leads you.

Date: _____

_____
_____
_____
_____
_____

Date: _____

_____
_____
_____
_____
_____

Date: _____

_____
_____
_____
_____
_____

Date: _____

_____
_____
_____
_____
_____
_____

"Hope is a renewable option: If you run out of it at the end of the day, you get to start over in the morning." **Barbara Kingsolver**

JOY

Nehemiah 8:10 - *"The joy of the Lord is your strength."*

REAWAKEN with Young Living's **Joy**, the eleventh oil in *Reboot.* Joy is a blend of essential oils containing the following: Bergamot, Ylang-Ylang, Geranium, Lemon, Coriander, Tangerine, Jasmine, Roman Chamomile, Palmarosa and Rose.
Item #3372 - 15 ml bottle - $44.75 / $58.88
Cost per drop: $0.18 / $0.24

Apply 1 – 2 drops of Joy to your non-dominant hand. With your pointer and middle finger, activate the oil three times in a clockwise motion. Apply **Joy** over the heart. **Joy** gives one a glorious feeling of self-love, confidence and creates a frequency around oneself of the energy of love, the true source of all healing. Through your nose, inhale **Joy** deeply and slowly. 5 - 10 times.

REALIGN with God's word by meditating on the following scriptures as Joy is being used:

1. Psalm 19:9 - *"The precepts of the Lord are right, giving joy to the heart. The commands of the Lord are radiant giving light to the eyes."*
2. John 15:11-13 - *"I have told you this so that my joy may be in you and that your joy may be complete. My command is this: Love each other as I have loved you. Greater love has no one than this: to lay down one's life for one's friends."*
3. Galatians 5:22 - *"But the fruit of the Spirit is love, joy, peace, forbearance, kindness, goodness, faithfulness, gentleness and self-control. Against such things, there is no law."*
4. Romans 15:13 - *"May the God of hope fill you with all joy and peace as you trust in him, so that you may overflow with hope by the power of the Holy Spirit."*

REAFFIRM: I am _____
(Put your full, given name here)

As you breathe **Joy** from your hands, think say and feel the following affirmations: *I am love. I am loved. I am lovable. My heart is full of joy and love.*

REFLECT: Record your own scriptures, thoughts, emotions, or prayers here as the Holy Spirit leads you.

Date: _____

_____
_____
_____
_____
_____
_____

Date: _____

_____
_____
_____
_____
_____
_____

Date: _____

_____
_____
_____
_____
_____
_____

Date: _____

_____
_____
_____
_____
_____
_____

"Joy is a net of love by which you can catch souls." **Mother Teresa**

PRESENT TIME

Romans 13:11 - "And do this, understanding the present time: The hour has already come for you to wake up from your slumber because our salvation is nearer now than when we first believed."

REAWAKEN with Young Living's **Present Time** is the twelfth oil in *Reboot*. **Present Time** is a blend of essential oils containing the following: Sweet Almond Oil, Bitter Orange, Black Spruce and Ylang-Ylang.
Item #3396 - 5 ml bottle - $92.50 / $121.71
Cost per drop: $1.23 / $1.62

Apply 1-2 drops of **Present Time** to your non-dominant hand. With your pointer and middle finger, activate the oil three times in a clockwise motion. Apply **Present Time** on the thymus in a circular clockwise motion. The thymus is the point on your body that you would touch if you were to point to yourself. Tap yourself slowly at this location three times as if to bring yourself to an awareness of NOW. **Present Time** helps bring you into the present moment, so you can let go of the past, stop worrying about the future and **be fully present now.** Through your nose, inhale Present **Time** deeply and slowly 5 – 10 times.

REALIGN with God's word by meditating on the following scriptures as **Present Time** is used:

1. Lamentations 3:22-23 - *"Because of the LORD's great love we are not consumed, for his compassions never fail. They are new every morning; great is your faithfulness."*
2. Psalm 118:24 - *"This is the day the Lord has made; We will rejoice and be glad in it."*
3. Matthew 6:34a - *"...do not worry about tomorrow, for tomorrow will worry about itself."*
4. Romans 11:5 - *"So too, at the present time there is a remnant chosen by grace."*
5. 2 Corinthians 6:2 - *"For he says, "In the time of my favor I heard you, and in the day of salvation I helped you. I tell you, **now** is the time of God's favor, **now** is the day of salvation."*

REAFFIRM: I am _____
(Put your full, given name here)

As you breathe **Present Time** from your hands, think, say, and feel the following affirmations: *I am fully present now. I am awake. I let go of the past and the future.*

REFLECT Record your own scriptures, thoughts, emotions, or prayers here as the Holy Spirit leads you.

Date: _____
_____
_____
_____
_____
_____
_____

Date: _____
_____
_____
_____
_____
_____
_____

Date: _____
_____
_____
_____
_____
_____
_____

Date: _____
_____
_____
_____
_____
_____
_____
_____

"Yesterday is history, tomorrow is a mystery, today is a gift of God, which is why we call it the present." **Bill Keane**

SARA

1 Peter 5:7 - *"Cast all your anxiety on Him, because he cares for you."*

REAWAKEN with Young Living's **SARA**, the thirteenth essential oil blend in *Reboot* and contains the following essential oils: Sweet Almond Oil, Ylang Ylang, Geranium, Lavender, Orange, Cedarwood, Blue Cypress, Davana, Lime, Jasmine, Rose, Matricaria, Blue Tansy, Grapefruit, Tangerine, Spearmint, Lemon, Ocotea, and White Lotus.
Item #3417 - 5 ml bottle - $27.50 / $36.18
Cost per drop: $0.37 / $0.48

Apply 1 – 2 drops of **SARA** to your non-dominant hand. With your pointer and middle finger, activate the oil three times in a clockwise motion. Apply **SARA** to each energy center, in and around your navel and across your chest. **SARA** may enable you to relax and to release the memory of traumatic experiences, especially those related to sexual abuse or ritual abuse. Smell **SARA** deeply and slowly 5 – 10 times.

REALIGN - Because this step is very personal, no scriptures are suggested. Meditate on scriptures that the Lord brings to your mind and the direction He gives for releasing emotions. Record them below.

_____
_____
_____
_____
_____
_____
_____
_____
_____
_____
_____
_____
_____
_____

REAFFIRM: I am _____

(Put your full, given name here)

As you breathe **SARA** from your hands, think, say, and feel the following affirmations: *I am safe. I am protected. I am treasured. I am whole. I am clean. I am light.*

REFLECT: Record your own scriptures, thoughts, emotions, or prayers here as the Holy Spirit leads you.

Date: _____

_____

_____

_____

_____

_____

Date: _____

_____

_____

_____

_____

_____

_____

Date: _____

_____

_____

_____

_____

_____

_____

Date: _____

_____

_____

_____

_____

_____

_____

"Your value doesn't decrease based on someone's inability to see your worth."
Unknown

WHITE ANGELICA

Psalm 91:11 - *"For he will command his angels concerning you to guard you in all your ways."*

REAWAKEN with Young Living's **White Angelica**, the fourteenth and final oil in *Reboot.* White Angelica is a blend of essential oils containing the following: Sweet Almond Oil, Bergamot, Myrrh, Geranium, Sacred Sandalwood, Ylang-Ylang, Coriander and Black Spruce, Melissa, Hyssop and Rose.
Item #3432 - 5 ml bottle - $30.00 / $39.47
Cost per drop: $0.40 / $0.53

Apply 1 – 2 drops of **White Angelica** in your non-dominant hand. With your pointer and middle finger, activate the oil three times in a clockwise motion. Apply **White Angelica** to the top of your head, shoulders and down your arms. **White Angelica** strengthens and fortifies one's aura, may generate a feeling of protection and an awareness of your potential. As the final oil in the emotion release protocol, it supports all that has taken place and prepares you to search inward for strength and to proceed with life and to search upward for the true source of love and light. Through your nose, inhale **White Angelica** deeply and slowly 5 – 10 times.

REALIGN with God's word by meditating on the following scriptures as **White Angelica** is being used:

1. Proverbs 4:23 - *"Above all else, guard your heart for everything you do flows from it."*
2. Psalm 5:11- *"But let all who take refuge in you be glad; let them ever sing for joy. Spread your protection over them, that those who love your name may rejoice in you."*
3. Ephesians 3:20 - *"Now to him who is able to do immeasurably more than all we ask or imagine, according to his power that is at work within us."*
4. Ephesians 6:11 - *"Put on the full armor of God, so that you can take your stand against the devil's schemes."*

REAFFIRM: I am _____

(Put your full, given name here)

As you breathe **White Angelica** from your hands, meditate on, believe, and feel the following affirmations: *I am strong. I am shielded. I am protected. I am positive.*

REFLECT: Record your own scriptures, thoughts, emotions, or prayers here as the Holy Spirit leads you.

Date: _____

_____
_____
_____
_____
_____

Date: _____

_____
_____
_____
_____
_____

Date: _____

_____
_____
_____
_____
_____

Date: _____

_____
_____
_____
_____
_____

Finally, brothers and sisters, whatever is true, whatever is noble, whatever is right, whatever is pure, whatever is lovely, whatever is admirable—if anything is excellent or praiseworthy—think about such things. **Philippians 4:8**

What to Expect AFTER *Reboot*

1. When possible, leave the *Reboot* essential oils on for 12 – 24 hours and drink plenty of water (with Lemon EO).
2. Rest. Relax. Give yourself permission to do as little as possible for the remainder of the day.
3. Be kind to yourself. Be kind to those around you.
4. Be aware that emotional release may take place several hours or even days after this session. Emotional release may come with tears or irritability.
5. If you experience irritability, avoid discussions or arguments that would escalate.
6. Expect deep relaxation and sweet peace.
7. *Reboot* again in 2 - 4 weeks or as the Holy Spirit would lead you.
8. **I would love to hear your *Reboot* testimonies! Send your testimony to RebootNow14@gmail.com.** With your permission, I will publish them on the testimonials page to encourage others to *Reboot*. (Only first names would be used).
9. Join our private *Reboot* group on Facebook for ongoing support, encouragement, and videos. Email RebootNow14@gmail.com to request an invitation.

I cannot stress enough how <u>important it is to replace toxic emotions, thoughts, and behaviors with the truth</u>. It is so important to use the Realign and Reaffirm steps, so you can fill your mind and heart with Truth and positive affirmations.

"When an impure spirit comes out of a person, it goes through arid places seeking rest and does not find it. Then it says, 'I will return to the house I left.' When it arrives, it finds the house unoccupied, swept clean and put in order. Then it goes and takes with it seven other spirits more wicked than itself, and they go in and live there. And the final condition of that person is worse than the first." Matthew 12:43 – 45.

Note: See the list of suggested Young Living essential oil blends that may be added to <u>Reboot</u> in the "Nuts & Bolts" section.

My Reboot Victories!

Applying the oils in **Reboot** repeatedly, helped me identify that my choice to flee, run, hide or leave was my "fight or flight" response engrained early on due to childhood trauma. As a five-year old child, terrified and unable to make sense out of the abuse before my innocent eyes, I *chose* "flight". This initial trauma and fear dictated a response pattern of running and hiding that was deeply etched in my brain. Every time this trauma was triggered, I spontaneously ran and hid out of fear. Fear was triggered when I was mad at my mom and ran away from home (to the back yard) at age nine. It was also fear that limited me from going too far. Fear

of rejection was triggered when I wanted to "fit in" as a teenager and under peer pressure began using alcohol and drugs. Fear of abandonment whispered lies in my ears to end my life when another boyfriend rejected me. Leaving was my only choice when a troubled, abusive marriage became too fearful. Distance and separation was my automatic default when job stress became what seemed unfair and unmanageable. For example, at a past job, during a discussion with a boss, he came out of his chair towards me as he was making a point. This triggered that buried trauma and my flight response took over. I went to the bathroom, locked the door, and cried. I responded the only way I knew and resigned that very afternoon. Removing myself was the only way I knew how to handle stressful or traumatic situations. I simply didn't have or *thought* I didn't have any other choice. Run and hide were the only tools in my toolbelt. Wrong or right, this perception was my reality. I perceived everything through the filter of fear. AND FEAR LIES. Using essential oils helped me pause and seek truth in each situation and to question what I was perceiving. I was able to ask myself, "Is it true?" I was able to identify patterns in my behavior. I discovered that many times I believed lies to be truth. As you, *Reboot*, ask God to reveal the truth to you. *"I am the way, the truth and the life."* John 14:6. Applying the oils in Reboot as tools for releasing emotions, allowed my past trauma to surface, to come into the light, so I was able to identify the unhealthy way(s) I dealt with fear. And at the same time, hand in hand with my faithful Father, He gave me the courage to release those negative emotions and the power to respond in healthy ways. **I no longer tell people that I am a "flight risk."**

FEAR – Face Everything and Run or
FEAR – Face Everything and RISE!

The essential oils in *Reboot* have supported healthy sleep patterns. I dream more often and upon waking, I remember my dreams. In dreams, relationships have been reconciled and then those reconciliations manifested quickly. In dreams, security has been regained, and I found my voice. In one particular dream, I was standing at an elevator with my mother and my grandson. Just as the elevator doors opened, my grandson stepped in and the elevator moved away like a conveyor belt. And at that very moment, my mother stepped forward and fell into the elevator shaft. I was instantly horrified and afraid, but instead of running and hiding, I screamed, "Help! Somebody help!" I know now that screaming for help in my dream was what fear didn't allow me to do when I was a child. I recovered my lost voice and I stayed.

This is how I know that essential oils are working every time we use them. We may not see results instantly, but the molecules in the essential oils are doing the work that God created them to do. Keep repeating *Reboot* until you see the fruit! Keep repeating *Reboot* until love wins! Keep repeating **Reboot** until you experience emotional wholeness. The truth in our heart *always* comes to the surface. Truth floats! We can push it down over and over. We can deny it, but it will always surface. The essential oils in **Reboot** gently reawaken memories, feelings, and trauma so you can look them square in the face, love them to death and then give them a proper burial. When you face those weaknesses, traumas, triggers, and fears with love in your tool belt, essential oils, and the power of the Holy Spirit, they will become your strengths and you will use those strengths to help other people with the same. *"Praise be to the God and Father of our Lord Jesus Christ, the Father of compassion and the God of all comfort, who comforts us in all our troubles, so that we can comfort those in any trouble with the comfort we ourselves receive from God. For just as we share abundantly in the sufferings of Christ, so also our comfort abounds through Christ."* 2 Corinthians 1:3-5.

Since using essential oils for emotional release, I have come to understand that every time trauma, hurt, anger or fear were triggered, it was a divine opportunity to put those feelings under the magnifying glass. It was an opportunity get up close and personal to fear. It was an opportunity to examine that emotion inside and out. It was an opportunity to wake up with eyes wide open to perceive what was real and true. It was an opportunity to choose love and be transformed by truth. Every fear faced is an opportunity to choose faith. Every lie that surfaces is an opportunity to choose truth. Every encounter with a person who had hurt me was an opportunity to choose forgiveness. *"Brothers and sisters, I do not consider myself yet to have taken hold of it. But one thing I do: forgetting what is behind and straining toward what is ahead, I press on toward the goal to win the prize for which God has called me heavenward in Christ Jesus."* Philippians 3:13-14.

"I thank my God every time I remember you. In all my prayers for all of you, I always pray with joy because of your partnership in the gospel from the first day until now, being confident of this, that he who began a good work in you will carry it on to completion until the day of Christ Jesus." Philippians 1:3-6.

Wouldn't you rather live fearless and free?

"Therefore, since we are surrounded by such a great cloud of witnesses, let us throw off everything that hinders and the sin that so easily entangles. And let us run with perseverance the race marked out for us, fixing our eyes on Jesus, the pioneer and perfecter of faith. For the joy set before him, he endured the cross, scorning its shame, and sat down at the right hand of the throne of God. Consider him who endured such opposition from sinners, so that you will not grow weary and lose heart." Hebrews 12:1-3

"Do you not know that in a race all the runners run, but only one gets the prize? Run in such a way as to get the prize. Everyone who competes in the games goes into strict training. They do it to get a crown that will not last, <u>but we do it to get a crown that will last forever.</u>" 1 Corinthians 9:24

"Now to him who is able to do immeasurably more than all we ask or imagine, according to his power that is at work within us, to Him be glory in the church and in Christ Jesus throughout all generations, for ever and ever! Amen."
Ephesians 3:20-21

SHARE R*EBOOT*!

I have met hundreds of people (family, friends, co-workers) who would benefit from Young Living essential oils and ***Reboot.*** You most likely have already thought of several people you could share ***Reboot*** with. In the spaces provided below, list at least twenty people who would benefit from using essential oils and ***Reboot***. Consider gifting a copy of ***Reboot*** to them, invite them to become a member of Young Living, or invite them to attend a ***Reboot*** class. If you are YL team leader, purchase ***Reboot*** in bulk and give ***Reboot*** to your entire team for their personal development. Make ***Reboot*** available at all your classes and events.

1. _____
2. _____
3. _____
4. _____
5. _____
6. _____
7. _____
8. _____
9. _____
10. _____
11. _____
12. _____
13. _____
14. _____
15. _____
16. _____
17. _____
18. _____
19. _____
20. _____

How to Host a REBOOT Class

1. **R – Reach Out**
2. **E – Educate - Emotions and EO**
3. **B – Buy the Book – REBOOT**
4. **O – Organize the Class**
5. **O – Oil up**
6. **T – Tell your REBOOT Story**
7. **S – Search for and Join our Private Facebook Group**

1. REACH OUT
   a. Advertise your *Reboot* Class on Social Media
   b. Call, text or email your YL Team
   c. Personally, invite family, friends, co-workers, people you know that are experiencing or have experienced a difficult situation (death, divorce, illness, trauma).

2. EDUCATE
   a. Share information about emotions and how essential oils help.
   b. Use information from *Reboot* (Please credit my book).
   c. Provide information about purchasing Young Living *Reboot* oils.
   d. Offer a free *Reboot* class to participants who enroll with a Starter Bundle.

3. BUY THE BOOK - REBOOT
   a. Purchase enough REBOOT books so each member of your class has a copy and charge enough for your class to cover the cost of the book ($9.95) plus the cost of the oils ($30.00). A fair price for the class is $40.00-60.00. **Reboot is available on Amazon in paperback and Kindle.**

4. **ORGANIZE the Class**
   a. Order the oils needed to REBOOT.
   b. Choose a location that your participants have enough space to lay down if they choose to.
   c. Ask participants to bring a blanket or yoga mat for larger groups.
   d. Provide a bottled water for each participant or ask participants to bring their own.

5. **OIL UP**
   a. Instruct participants about holding a sacred space and voting everyone's victory and declare a no-judgment zone.
   b. Facilitator reads the Reawaken step and distributes the oils to each participant.
   c. Facilitator reads the Realign and Reaffirm steps.
   d. Facilitator prompts participants to take time to Reflect. Provide pens if needed.

6. **TELL YOUR REBOOT STORY**
   a. Share your own REBOOT experience.
   b. Ask participants to share a testimony.
   c. Discuss pages 72-75 so participants know how to get their own REBOOT oils and who to get them from.
   d. Share a (five-star) review on Amazon about REBOOT and/or send a testimony to RebootNow14@gmail.com.

7. **Search for and join our private *Reboot* Facebook Group**
   a. Invite anyone who has a copy of this book to join. **Questions must be answered to enter.**
   b. Get on-going support and encouragement.
   c. Find a loving community.
   d. Ask questions.
   e. Use the author-led videos in your classes.
   f. Additional Reboot items: ***Reboot*** bookmarks and bracelets. Coming soon: ***Reboot*** Journal

A Few Nuts & Bolts

The total *wholesale* cost (Subscribe to save or Brand Partner) to purchase all fourteen oils in *Reboot* is $749.50. The total *retail* cost (customer price) of all fourteen oils in *Reboot* is $986.17. Enrolling as a Brand Partner and buying the essential oils at the wholesale price (24% off retail) in *Reboot* saves $236.67. This more than covers the cost of a Starter Bundle! You can save money by purchasing all fourteen oils on Young Living's free, Loyalty Rewards program. (see Appendix 4 to learn more about Loyalty Rewards and an example of how to purchase all fourteen oils in nine months).

The approximate cost of the essential oil drops for one person to participate in a *Reboot* class is $20.00 to $30.00. This will vary due to the number of drops used in each step. Licensed massage therapists, professionals and those trained in emotional release may charge according to their own fee schedules.

Additional oils you may choose to add to *Reboot* - Acceptance, Awaken, Clarity, Highest Potential, Into the Future, Magnify Your Purpose, Peace & Calming, Sacred Mountain, Surrender, and/or Trauma Life.

Note: Prices are taken from the Young Living 2020 Product Guide and are listed wholesale/retail. Young Living may increase prices at any time. Some of the Young Living formulas may change. The cost per drop is listed wholesale then retail and is based on 75 drops in a 5 ml bottle and 250 drops in a 15 ml bottle. Some oils may have more or less drops depending on the viscosity of the oil or the addition of a carrier oil as noted on the label of each bottle.

Appendix 1 - The Limbic System

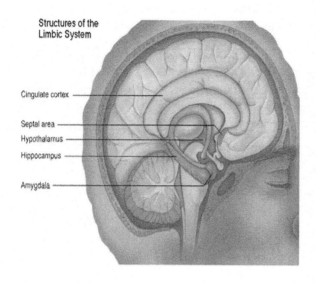

Structures of the Limbic System

Cingulate cortex

Septal area
Hypothalamus
Hippocampus

Amygdala

Amygdala - almond-shaped mass of nuclei involved in emotional responses, hormonal secretions, and memory. The amygdala is responsible for fear conditioning or the associative learning process by which we learn to fear something.

Cingulate Gyrus- a fold in the brain involved with sensory input concerning emotions and the regulation of aggressive behavior.

Hippocampus - a tiny nub that acts as a memory indexer -- sending memories out to the appropriate part of the cerebral hemisphere for long-term storage and retrieving them when necessary.

Hypothalamus - about the size of a pearl, this structure directs a multitude of important functions. It wakes you up in the morning and gets the adrenaline flowing. The hypothalamus is also an important emotional center, controlling the molecules that make you feel exhilarated, angry, or unhappy.

Olfactory Cortex- receives sensory information from the olfactory bulb and is involved in the identification of odors.

Thalamus - a large, dual lobed mass of gray matter cells that relay sensory signals to and from the spinal cord and the cerebrum. Credit: https://www.thoughtco.com/limbic-system-anatomy-373200

Appendix 2
Essential Oils - Phenols, Sesquiterpenes, Monoterpenes
(This is not an exhaustive list)

Phenols Scrub	Sesquiterpenes Deprogram	Monoterpenes Reprogram
Wintergreen 97%	Cedarwood 95%	Grapefruit 93%
Anise 90%	Patchouli 85%	Orange 90%
Clove 77%	Sandalwood 83%	Balsam Fir 83%
Basil 76%	Ginger 77%	Angelica 80%
Fennel 72%	Blue Cypress 73%	Frankincense 78%
Oregano 70%	Myrrh 65%	Cypress 76%
Thyme 50%	Vetiver 59%	Nutmeg 68%
	G. Chamomile 54%	Lime 62%
	Spikenard 52%	Bergamot 55%
		Juniper 54%
		Tea Tree 52%
		Pine 51%
		Black Pepper 50%
		Blue Tansy 50%
		Dill 50%

Credit: The Chemistry of Essential Oils Made Simple David Steward Ph.D., D.N.M pgs. 569, 571, 572 (portions of)

Appendix 3
7 Energy Centers Diagram

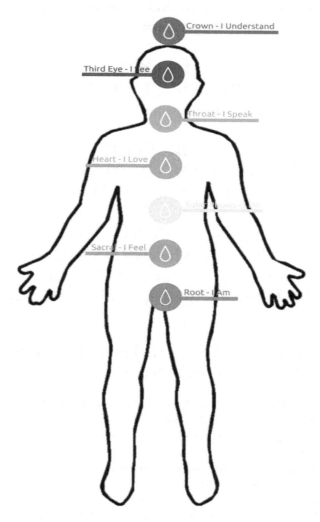

Are Chakras New Age? **by David Stewart, PhD**
Raindrop Messenger Archives: Volume 11 Number 4 Winter
Edition 2013

http://www.raindroptraining.com/messenger/v11n4.html#newage

Appendix 4

How to Purchase *Reboot* Oils on Young Living's Loyalty Rewards Program

"GOOD"
RETAIL CUSTOMER
Best oils on the planet at retail prices

"BETTER"
BRAND PARTNER
Best oils on the planet at 24% off retail

"BEST"
LOYALTY REWARDS MEMBER
Subscribe to save, Earn up to 25% back, Loyalty Gifts, Free/reduced shipping, Loyalty Exclusives

Benefits of Young Living's FREE Loyalty Rewards Program (formerly Essential Rewards)

1. **Loyalty Rewards is the BEST way to be a wholesale member of Young Living.**
2. Only one requirement: Purchase a minimum of 50 PV per month on subscribe to save.
3. Select only the products you want by changing your cart contents each month.
4. Change your ship date if needed.
5. Earn PV points: For the first three months you order on Essential Rewards, you get 10% back of your total PV purchased. For months 4 - 24, you get 20% back, and months 25 and beyond, you get 25% back to spend on products under the *Shop* button.

6. Free and/or reduced shipping fees.
7. Choose Loyalty Rewards kits which offer more savings.
8. Exclusive monthly promotions for Loyalty Rewards members and FREE products at 100 PV, 190 PV, 250 PV, 300 PV and sometimes 400 PV thresholds.
9. Receive FREE loyalty gifts at 3, 6, 9 and 12 months when you stay enrolled as a Loyalty Rewards member.

Example: *Reboot* Oils Purchased on Loyalty Rewards in Nine Months

Month	Oil /Oil Blend	Wholesale	Percent	PV Earned
1	Forgiveness	$56.25	10%	$5.62
2	Release & Grounding	$40.75 + 19.00=$59.75	10%	$5.97
3	Inner Child & SARA	$31.75 + 27.50=$59.25	10%	$5.93
4	Hope & Believe	$61.00 + $40.00=$101.00	20%	$20.20
5	Harmony	$74.50	20%	$14.90
6	3 Wise Men	$94.00	20%	$18.80
7	Present Time	$92.50	20%	$18.50
8	Joy & Valor	$44.75 + $41.25=$86.00	20%	$17.20
9	Sacred Frankincense & White Angelica	$96.25+$30.00 =$126.25	20%	$25.25
Total Loyalty PV points earned to use on other purchases or oils used in *Reboot*				**$132.37**

Note: *Suggested* order above is for *minimum* Loyalty requirements & *maximum* PV earned. Prices shown are from the June 2020 pricelist.

*Save more money!! You may also consider purchasing the Feelings Kit which bundles six of the **_Reboot_** oils: Valor, Harmony, Forgiveness, Release, Present Time, and Inner Child. Item #3125 - Wholesale: $188.25 / Retail: $247.70.

Start Your Young Living Wellness Journey!

Reconnect with the person who shared Young Living Essential Oils or **Reboot** with you and use their member referral number when you enroll as a wholesale member of Young Living. If that was me, begin your wholesale membership by visiting my website: **www.Oily Baalievers.com** and click on the "Order Now" button. I would be honored and blessed to support you as you begin your Young Living Essential Oil journey!

Choose a Starter Bundle. Decide if you want to be a GOOD, BETTER or BEST member of Young Living. The BEST way to become a member of Young Living is by selecting Young Living's FREE Loyalty Rewards membership during your enrollment. Choose what you want, when you want it, and it will be delivered right to your door every month.

Need help? Contact me!

Oily Baa-lievers
Kathleen Rodin
Chief Executive Oily Officer
YL Independent Distributor
Member #2176680
Email: RebootNow14@gmail.com
Web: www.OilyBaalievers.com
FB: www.facebook.com/kathysoilpub

Are you a believer in Jesus?
If you aren't sure or would like to be, keep reading and pray this prayer.

1. **Consider** - *"For it is by grace you have been saved, through faith- and this is not from yourselves, it is the gift of God, not by works, so that no one can boast."* Ephesians 2:8-9. *"Once you were alienated from God and were enemies in your minds because of your evil behavior. But now he has reconciled you by Christ's physical body through death to present you holy in his sight, without blemish and free from accusation."* Colossians 1:21-22. *"I am the good shepherd. The good shepherd lays down his life for the sheep."* John 10:11

2. **Confess** - *"For all have sinned and fall short of the glory of God."* Romans 3:23. *"If we confess our sins, he is faithful and just and will forgive us our sins and purify us from all unrighteousness."* 1 John 8-10.

3. **Believe** - *"Very truly I tell you, whoever hears my word and believes him who sent me has eternal life and will not be judged but has crossed over from death to life."* John 5:24. *"For God so loved the world that he gave his one and only begotten son that whoever believes in him shall not perish but have eternal life."* John 3:16.

4. **Receive** - Pray this prayer: *"Father God, I have sinned. I have not obeyed your Word. I have tried to run my own life. I have ignored you and your will for me. I have tried to decide for myself what is right and wrong. I am lost and deserve your wrath and punishment unless you save me. Thank you for sending your Son, the Lord Jesus Christ, to pay for my sin. Thank you for raising Him from the dead and giving Him authority over my life. I receive Him as my Savior and Lord. I receive your gift of eternal life in Christ. I will turn from my sinful life to serve you. Amen."*

"Believe in the Lord Jesus Christ and you will be saved." Acts 16:3

© **No part of this publication may be reproduced, stored in a retrieval system, or transmitted in any form or by any means without prior, written permission of the author/publisher.**